ODPM *Circular 03/2005*
Office of the Deputy Prime Minister
Eland House, Bressenden Place, London SWIE 5DU

21 March 2005

CHANGES OF USE OF BUILDINGS AND LAND

The Town & Country Planning (Use Classes) Order 1987

INTRODUCTION

1. The Statutory Instrument 2005/84, which amends the *Town & Country Planning (Use Classes) Order 1987*, comes into force on 21st April 2005. The *Town and Country Planning (General Permitted Development) Order 1995* is also amended by Statutory Instrument 2005/85 to reflect the changes to the Use Classes Order. These amendments follow extensive consultation about the changes considered necessary to reflect current circumstances and to ensure the Use Classes Order remains an effective tool for delivering the Government's planning policies.

2. Circular 13/87, which gives advice on the 1987 Use Classes Order, is hereby cancelled. This Circular, provides a guide to the Use Classes Order as amended by SI 2005/85. It should, however, be remembered that although this Circular gives guidance amounting to an interpretation of the Order, only the courts can interpret the law authoritatively.

BACKGROUND

3. Under the *Town and Country Planning Act 1990*, development control extends not only to new building work but also to changes in use of buildings or land. Accordingly, planning permission is normally required for material changes of use. Judgment of what constitutes a material change of use is a matter of fact and degree to be determined in each case.

4. Certain uses of land are so similar, in planning land-use terms, that to require planning permission to change between them might be considered as overly burdensome. It serves no-one's interest to require planning permission in such cases.

5. Therefore, in order to relieve the planning system of a large number of unnecessary applications, the 1990 Act excludes from the definition of development (and hence from planning control) any change of use where both the existing and proposed uses fall within the same single class in the order.

THE AMENDED ORDER

6.   The aim of the amended Order is twofold:-

   (i)   to ensure that the scope of each class accurately reflects the impact on the environment of that class whilst remaining wide enough to encompass the changing needs of a diverse economy; and

   (ii)   to deliver the Government's planning policies more effectively.

7.   The First Secretary of State considers that effective control must be retained over changes of use that would have a material impact, in land-use planning terms, on local amenity or the environment, or would encourage development in locations that would be in conflict with national planning policy.

8.   The changes introduced by the amended Order are principally of interest to owners of business properties, in particular those in the food and drink and nightclub industries. There are now three classes formed by the disaggregation of the former A3: *Food and Drink* use class. In addition, nightclubs, previously not specified in the Order, are confirmed as not being in any class of the Order, and are therefore *sui generis* (of its own kind). These changes have been made in order to enable local planning authorities to manage the mix of uses in town centres, to tackle the environmental impact of the evening economy and to clarify the position on the classification of nightclubs under the 1987 Order.

9.   The amended Order also clarifies certain uses which have developed as a result of technological and market changes. Internet cafes are defined as an A1 classification. Retail warehouse clubs involving the sale or display for sale of good only to members of a club are confirmed as *sui generis*. Motor vehicle showrooms are to remain outside the use classes order, as before, although the previous permitted development rights which allowed a change of use to A1: *Shops* is removed from the *Town and Country Planning (General Permitted Development) Order 1995* (the GPDO).

10. The amended Order retains the four broad classifications of the 1987 Order. These generally correspond with (A) high street or shopping area uses; (B) other business and industrial uses; (C) residential uses; and (D) social and community uses of a non-residential kind.

GENERAL POINTS

11. Besides the advice in paragraphs 28-86 on the details of the classes, local planning authorities may find the following general points helpful.

- **Primary purpose**

12. The Courts have held that the first thing to consider in determining whether a material change of use has occurred (or will occur) is the existing primary use of the land. Each case will always be a matter for individual determination by fact and degree. In particular, local planning authorities will need to take into consideration more than just the amount of floor space occupied by the different uses. For example, in the case of a premises which incorporates restaurant use as well as pub or bar use, the local planning

authority will need to determine whether the existing primary use of the premises is as a restaurant (A3), or as a drinking establishment (A4), or a mixed use. This will depend on such matters as whether customers come primarily to eat, or drink, or both. It is the main purpose of that use that is to be considered.

- **Mixed uses**

13. Where the primary use of land or premises is a mixture of different uses, such mixed use does not fall into any of the classes set out in the amended Order. The use will therefore be *sui generis*.

14. Planning Permission is not always required for the change of use from one mixed use to another. The question is whether or not the change of use is material, in planning terms. Where the change of use does not amount to a material change, there will be no development, and no need to obtain planning permission.

- **Sub-division and intensification of uses**

15. As a result of the *Housing and Planning Act 1986*, and Article 4 of the amended Order, planning permission is not required for the sub-division of premises other than dwelling houses, provided that both the existing and proposed uses fall within the same use class.

16. Intensification of a use within a class in the Order has been held by the courts as not to constitute development unless and until its effect is to take the use outside of that class altogether.

17. Taken together, these points mean that if a building used for purposes falling within a particular use class were to be sub-divided, without physical works amounting to development, and each of the units was to be used for purposes which also fell within the same class, planning permission is unlikely to be required, even though any associated intensification might be a material change of use.

18. On the other hand, planning permission will be required if subdivision of a building used for a purpose not within any use class was accompanied by intensification amounting to a material change of use. Planning permission will also be required if subdivision of a building were to result in the primary use of any resulting part not continuing within the same use class as the use to which the whole building was put before the subdivision.

19. The effect of Article 4 of the 1987 Order is to ensure that development requiring planning permission arises whenever a dwelling house is sub-divided. Where a house with a separate "granny annex" or lodge occupied together with it is regarded as a single dwelling house, planning permission will only be required to occupy house and lodge as separate dwelling houses.

- **Unimplemented consents**

20. The Act provides that a change from one use to another within the same class is not to be regarded as development. This means that a use has to be begun before the Order can have effect. The question of whether or not a use has begun is a matter of fact to be determined in each separate case.

21. When the amended Order comes into effect, on 21st April 2005, there will be a number of extant, but unimplemented, planning permissions for development which refer to use classes contained in the previous Order. For example, an A2 premises may have existing but unimplemented planning consent for a change of use to an A3 use class, implying the former A3: *Food and Drink* use class.

22. Unless otherwise indicated, a planning permission is interpreted on the basis of the Use Classes Order in force at the time that the consent was given. Therefore, using the example above, if an unimplemented consent for an A3 use was granted before 21st April 2005, it will continue to permit changes of use to all of the former uses permitted by the former A3, including drinking establishments and takeaway uses.

23. Planning consents granted after 21st April 2005 will, however, be interpreted on the basis of the amended Use Classes Order. In cases where local planning authorities are processing applications for A3 uses which were received prior to 21st April 2005, they will need to clarify the precise use for which consent is being sought before determining such applications.

- **Reclassification of use as a result of the amended Order**

24. After the amended UCO comes into effect, uses that previously fell into the former A3: *Food and Drink* use class will fall into one of the new use classes: A3, A4 or A5. Re-classification of a use does not amount to development within the meaning of the 1990 Act.

- **Conditions**

25. *Circular 11/95 - The use of conditions in planning permission* makes it clear that there is a presumption against conditions designed to restrict future changes of use which, by virtue of the Use Classes Order or the General Permitted Development Order, would not otherwise constitute development. For example, whilst it is a change of use for an A4 use, such as pub or bar, to be converted into an A3 use, such as a restaurant or café, it is one that is permitted under the General Permitted Development Order, and as a general rule conditions should not be imposed which prevent it. The Secretary of State will regard the imposition of such conditions as unreasonable unless there is clear evidence that in the particular circumstances the uses excluded could have serious adverse affects on the environment or on amenity not susceptible to other control.

26. If, exceptionally, conditions restricting changes of use are justified they should be so drafted so as to prohibit a change to a particular potentially unacceptable use or uses, rather than in terms which require future approval of any change of use at all. Authorities should always give proper, adequate and intelligible reasons for the conditions they impose.

- **Excluded uses**

27. Article 3(6) of the Use Classes Order provides that certain uses are not within in any class of the Order. Such uses are *sui generis*. This does not mean that such uses will always be regarded as environmentally undesirable and thus liable to be refused permission, but rather that in most places where such uses are proposed, consideration by local planning authorities will be justified. The list of omissions is not exhaustive; many uses do not

clearly fall within any class and new types of use are constantly emerging. The Courts have held that it is not necessary to go to extreme lengths to identify a class for every use.

THE CLASSES OF THE AMENDED ORDER

28. The following paragraphs are a brief commentary on the classes, including the new ones.

Part A

29. This part of the amended Order comprises five classes, covering uses which will generally be found in shopping areas. The character and vitality of shopping centres depend on many factors, such as size, location, access, number and range of shops and other facilities, and thus the number of people who can be attracted. Service uses, including cafés and restaurants, may contribute to their vitality.

30. The separate use classes will enable the local planning authority to exert more influence over the broad composition of shopping areas in terms of land use. In particular, the disaggregation of the former A3: *Food and Drink* use class will give local planning authorities a greater degree of precision in making development control decisions, with a clearer view of the likely and continuing impact of those uses.

31. The new use classes are intended to enable local planning authorities to secure a satisfactory balance in an area between the numbers of restaurants/cafés, pubs/bars, and takeaways/fast food premises. This will help to ensure that one use does not predominate to the detriment of local amenity or the vitality of the area. Local planning authorities will need to treat applications on their merits with regard to the potential environmental impacts. However, the new, more specific, use classes will mean greater clarity in determining the effects on amenity of particular uses.

32. In addition, the amended Order has preserved the separation, established in the 1987 Order, of High Street office uses, i.e. offices serving the public, from other office uses not directly serving the public.

- **Class A1: *Shops***

33. The first class in Part A of the 1987 Order is a *shops* class. It is largely unchanged from the previous version of the Order, but is expanded to include internet cafés (premises where the primary purpose is to provide access for members of the public to the internet). Internet cafes are considered to provide a valuable service to the public and are therefore a valid high street feature. Further guidance on internet cafes is given below (see paragraph 37). Premises where goods are received for washing or cleaning are included in the shops class, but not premises in which the cleaning or washing of clothes or fabrics is carried out in coin-operated machines – launderettes or dry-cleaners – which, by virtue of article 3(6) are excluded from any use class. Shops for the sale of motor vehicles are also specifically excluded from any use class. Post offices, but not postal sorting offices, are within the shops class.

Sandwich bars

34. As indicated above in paragraph 12, in considering where individual uses fall, it is the primary purpose that should be considered. A sandwich bar does not necessarily cease to be in the shops class merely because, for example, it also sells a limited amount of hot drinks, hot soup or food that is heated up. Similarly, it is possible for a few sandwich bar customers to eat on the premises, including at tables within or outside their establishments (e.g. on the forecourt) without involving a material change of use. Provided that this is only an ancillary part of their business, the classification of the business as a sandwich bar would rightly remain in the A1: *Shops* use class where the retail sales element is the primary purpose.

Car Showrooms

35. The use of premises for the sale or display for sale of motor vehicles remains excluded from classification. However, the GPDO is amended so that a change of use from such premises to an A1: *Shops* use is no longer permitted. In addition, so as to align planning guidance with case law[1], retail warehouse clubs are also excluded from classification.

Coffee Shops

36. Coffee shops will need to be considered on a case by case basis. Whether their primary purpose is as a shop, i.e. premises for the sale of beverages to be taken away, or as a café, where the primary purpose is consumption of beverages on the premises, or indeed whether it is a mix of both uses.

Internet Cafés

37. Internet cafés, also called cyber cafés, are premises whose main function is the provision of internet access facilities, although the majority of these premises may have ancillary café facilities. The amended Order classifies these premises as A1 (premises where the primary purpose is to provide access for members of the public to the internet). However, as with sandwich bars and coffee shops, it is the primary purpose that needs to be considered. The availability of hot and cold drinks, and perhaps a separate area for consumption (to avoid spillage and damage to expensive machinery) will not, in itself, invalidate the A1 status of the internet café provided that the café element is an ancillary aspect of the business. Similarly, a café will not be classified as an internet café on the basis of a relatively few computer terminals available for use by customers.

• Class A2: *Financial and Professional Services*

38. The A2: *Financial and Professional services* use class remains unchanged from the 1987 Order. This class is designed to allow flexibility within a sector which is very much a part of the established shopping street scene, and which is expanding and diversifying. It enables planning control to be maintained over proposals involving the conversion of shops for purposes other than for the retail sale of goods, while permitting free interchange within a wide range of professional and financial service uses which the public now expects to find in shopping areas.

---

1 3R v. Thurrock Borough Council and others, exparte Tesco and others – October 1993

- ### Class A3: *Restaurants and Cafes*

39. The new A3: *Restaurants and Cafes* class is one of three new classes, created from the disaggregation of the former A3: *Food and Drink* use class formed in the 1987 Order. This new class is designed specifically for restaurants and cafés, i.e. places where the primary purpose is the sale and consumption of food and light refreshments on the premises.

40. Many premises have a service area in which meals are served as well as a bar area for the serving or consumption of drinks. Nevertheless, the serving of drink in a restaurant is often ancillary to the purchase and consumption of a meal. The primary purpose is what needs to be considered in determining whether a particular premises is classified in the A3 use class, or is a mixed use.

41. A restaurant whose trade is primarily in-house dining but which has ancillary bar use will be in Class A3. Where the pub or bar activity is a minor component of the business and will not affect environmental amenity, it will treated as ancillary to the primary (restaurant) use of the premises. Such matters will be decided on the basis of fact and degree in each case.

42. Premises in the A3 class have a permitted change of use to both the A1: *Shops* and A2: *Financial/Professional services* use class but not to any other use class.

- ### Class A4: *Drinking Establishments*

43. The new A4: *Drinking Establishments* class is the second of three new classes replacing the former A3: *Food and Drink* class. It caters specifically for pubs and bars, i.e. places where the primary purpose is the sale and consumption of alcoholic drink on the premises.

44. Premises in this category, by virtue of Part 3 of the amended GPDO, have a permitted change of use to new A3: *restaurant and cafe* premises, as well as to both the A1: *Shops* and A2: *Financial & Professional Services* uses.

45. In each of these new classes, the existing primary use will be crucial in determining the appropriate classification. In making a determination as to the correct classification, some account may be taken of factors such as: whether the majority of customers on the premises are consuming alcoholic liquor exclusively; whether there is a public house licence; and whether there is any obligation or expectation for customers to consume a meal.

46. Where it is evident that the primary use of the premises is the purchase and consumption of alcoholic liquor on the premises, the use class will normally be A4, irrespective of the square footage which may be given over to dining as an additional service, or the revenue derived from that function.

- ### Class A5: *Hot Food Takeaways*

47. The A5 class is the last of the newly-created classes from the former *Food and Drink* class. It caters specifically for takeaways and fast-food premises, i.e. premises where the existing primary purpose is the sale of hot food to take away.

48.   Takeaways are differentiated from restaurants because they raise different environmental issues, such as litter, longer opening hours, and extra traffic and pedestrian activity, from those generally raised by A3: *Restaurant and Café* uses. With A3 uses, any takeaway food sold on an ancillary basis is usually taken home for consumption.

49.   It is recognised that many hot food takeaways exist on premises which are of considerable size in square footage terms - considerably larger, in some cases, than other restaurants within the locality which are classified as A3. The existence of tables and chairs within a hot food outlet does not, in itself, make the premises a restaurant where the takeaway element is predominant.

50.   Premises in this category are permitted a change of use to new A3: *Restaurant and Cafe* premises, as well as to both the A1: *Shops* and A2: *Finance and Professional Services* uses, but not to any other use.

Part B

51.   Part B of the Order remains unchanged.

•   **Class B1: *Businesses***

52.   Accordingly, B1 remains a business class which groups together many office and light industrial uses which are broadly similar in their environmental impact and puts them into a single class.

53.   Provided that the limitation specified in the class is satisfied, this class will also include other laboratories and studios and "high tech" uses spanning office, light industrial and research and development (for example, the manufacture of computer hardware and software, computer research and development, provision of consultancy services, and after-sales services, as well as micro-engineering, bio-technology and pharmaceutical research, development and manufacture), in either offices or light industrial premises, whichever are more suitable.

54.   The amended Order maintains the approach of considering whether a use is capable of being carried on within a residential area. All aspects of the use are considered against the criteria: noise, vibrations, smell, fumes, smoke, soot, ash, dust or grit. In this context, there will normally be no material change of use requiring planning permission until an intensification or change in the nature of the use is such that it would no longer satisfy the limitation specified in the class.

•   **Class B2: *General Industrial***

55.   The B2: *Industry* use class category remains unchanged. Accordingly, it covers a variety of industrial uses.

•   **Class B8: *Storage & Distribution***

56.   The B8: *Storage and Distribution* class is also unaffected by the amendments to the 1987 Order.

57. This class is defined by the character of the use of the land, not the appearance or description of a building. This class should not be used for the classification of retail warehouses where the main purpose is for the sale of goods direct to the public, which will generally fall within the A1: *Shops* class, however much floor space is used for storage.

Part C

58. Part C of the Order remains unchanged.

- ### Class C1: *Hotels*

59. The C1: *Hotels* use class remains unchanged from the original 1987 Order (as amended by *SI 1994/724* which removed hostels from this classification). The C1: *Hotels* class includes not only hotels, but also motels, bed and breakfast premises, boarding and guest houses. These are premises which provide a room as temporary accommodation on a commercial, fee-paying basis, where meals can be provided but where residential care is not provided. In addition, short-term (i.e. purchased at a nightly rate with no deposit against damage being required) self-contained accommodation, sometimes called Apart-Hotels, will also fall into this class.

Hostels

60. Hostels were excluded from the Use Classes Order in 1994 (by *SI 1994/724*) and are therefore *sui generis*.

61. There is no definition of 'hostel' within planning law. A hostel usually provides overnight or short-term accommodation which may be supervised, where people (including sometimes the homeless) can usually stay free or cheaply. Hostels may provide board, although some may provide facilities for self-catering. The element of supervision should not be relied upon as a determining factor but as a factor to take into account in consideration of the use class of the premises. Occasionally, hostels are used to provide longer-term accommodation, although it should be stressed that a hostel is not a residential care home, irrespective of any supervision it may have. If there is an element of care in the service provision, this might mean that the premises became a C2: *Residential Institutions* use.

62. The question of whether a premises is a hostel or another use is a matter of judgement to be determined on a fact and degree basis. In 1985, in the High Court judgement in the case of *Panayi v. Secretary of State for the Environment* and *Hackney LBC* [JPL 783], it was argued that the presence and use of some of the features below combined were sufficient to distinguish the use of the premises as that of a hostel.

- The presence of dormitories and/or communal or shared facilities.

- The use of the premises in accommodating specific categories of people, e.g., the young, or the homeless.

- Whether the premises are serviced and/or supervised.

- Whether payment is made by the local authority.

- Whether payment is on a nightly basis.

- Whether the residents are transient in the sense that they are 'placed' in the accommodation whilst awaiting accommodation elsewhere.

- The requirements of fire or safety certificates indicating the type of usage.

- The display of such notices or other indicators which may indicate the type of usage: e.g., fire certificates, public fire notices of use for staff and guests.

- **Class C2: *Residential Institutions***

63.   The C2: *Residential Institutions* class remains unchanged. Apart from educational establishments, the characteristic of the uses contained in this class that sets them apart from the C1: *Hotels* and C3: *Dwelling houses* use classes is, in the case of C1, the provision of personal care and treatment; and, in the case of C3, that the residents and staff do not form a single household. (Article 2 provides a specific definition of care for the purposes of this class.)

64.   The Secretary of State is aware of concern that residential care homes and nursing homes should not be permitted where they will be in place additional demands in already stretched essential services. However, it is important for local planning authorities to concentrate on the land-use planning considerations to be taken into account when considering a planning application for a change of use falling within this class.

65.   Unless they are managed or provided by a body constituted by an Act of Parliament or incorporated by Royal Charter, all private and voluntary homes (except residential care homes with three beds or less) have to be registered with the local social services authority or the district health authority. Registration can be refused on the grounds that the home would not provide adequate services or facilities reasonably required by residents or patients. The registering authorities may consult each other and the family practitioner committee about the provision of health and social services for residents. Therefore, among the land-use planning considerations local planning authorities will need to concern themselves mainly with the impact of a proposed institution on amenity and the environment. They should also avoid giving the impression that, if planning permission is granted, registration is likely to follow automatically. It is important that intending developers should discuss their proposals with the registration authority before investing money in them.

- **Class C3: *Dwelling Houses***

66.   The amended Order does not make any changes to class C3: *Dwelling houses*. This class groups together use as a *dwelling house*, whether or not the sole or main residence, by single person, any number of persons living together as a family, or by no more than 6 persons living together as a single household. The key element in the use of a dwelling house for non-family purposes is the concept of a single household. The single household concept will provide more certainty over the planning position of small group homes which play a major role in the Government's community care policy which is aimed at enabling disabled and mentally disordered people to live as normal lives as possible in touch with the community.

67.   In the case of small residential care homes or nursing homes, staff and residents will probably not live as a single household and the use will therefore fall into the residential institutions, regardless of the size of the home. Local planning authorities should include any resident care staff in their calculation of the number of people accommodated.

68.   This class not only includes families, or people living together under arrangements for provision of care, but also other groups of people, not necessarily related to each other, who chose to live on a communal basis as a single household.

69.   The term 'dwelling house' is not defined in the Use Classes Order. Nor is its definition limited, as in the GPDO 1995, so as to exclude flats. The question of whether a particular building is a dwelling house is therefore one of fact.

70.   The common feature of all premises which can generally be described as dwelling houses is that they are buildings that ordinarily afford the facilities required for day to day private domestic existence. It is recognised that unlikely or unusual buildings, such as churches or windmills, have been used as, or adapted to become, homes and dwelling houses. Whilst such premises may not be regarded as being dwelling houses in the traditional sense, they may be so classified for the purposes of the Use Classes Order.

71.   The criteria for determining whether the use of particular premises should be classified within the C3 use class include both the manner of the use and the physical condition of the premises. Premises can properly be regarded as being used as a single dwelling house where they are:

   •   a single, self-contained unit of occupation which can be regarded as being a separate 'planning unit,' distinct from any other part of the building containing them;

   •   designed, or adapted, for residential purposes - containing the normal facilities for cooking, eating and sleeping associated with use as a dwelling house;

   •   used as a dwelling, whether permanently or temporarily, by a single person, a family, or more than one person living together like a family, as a single household.

72.   This interpretation would exclude such uses as bed-sitting room accommodation if the occupants share some communal facilities within a building, such as a bathroom or lavatory. Here, the "planning unit" is likely to be the whole building in use for the purposes of multiple residential occupation, rather than each individual unit of accommodation.

73.   Sheltered housing developments will usually fall within the C3 class.

Houses in Multiple Occupation (HMOs)

74.   Planning legislation defines neither "multiple occupation" nor HMOs, as such, but as indicated above, relies on both the concept of a "single household" and "family" in making distinctions for land-use purposes.

75.   HMOs are unclassified by the Use Classes Order.

76. Although the control limit of six persons defines the scope of the C3 dwelling house classes, this does not imply that any excess of that number must constitute a breach of planning control. Where six people have lived together as a single household, there will subsequently be a material change of use only where the total number of residents increases to the point where it can be said that the use has intensified so as to become of a different character or the residents no longer live together as a single household.

77. Although the courts have provided some guidance on the definition of "one household" they have not yet considered what constitutes people "living together as a family". In *R v Kettering BC & English Churches Housing Group* (2002), the Court of Appeal, when considering what might be "one household" opined that the precise relationship between residents, although clearly a material consideration, was not necessarily determinative of the matter. This may well apply to any definition of "family" where there may be no legal relationship between the occupants. Factors such as the number of residents and the stability of the group will be material.

Working from home and live-work units

78. A fact and degree approach is also needed in determining when the carrying on of business activities in a dwelling house requires planning permission. The amended Order does not alter the current position: planning permission for working at home is not usually needed where the use of part of a dwelling house for business purposes does not change the overall character of its use as a residence. The *Step-By-Step Guide to Planning Permission for Small Business* contains more detailed advice about the planning issues to consider in relation to working from home.

79. Live/work units are often purpose-built premises, or purposely converted into such units. They are clearly a mix of residential and business uses which cannot be classified under a single class within the Use Classes Order and would therefore be *sui generis*.

Part D

80. Part D is largely unchanged, although nightclubs are confirmed as *sui generis*.

- ### Class D1: *Non-Residential Institutions*

81. The D1: *Non-residential Institutions* use class is unchanged.

82. The *Non-residential Institutions* class groups together buildings visited by the public for a wide range of purposes on a non-residential basis. It is intended to include day-centres (defined in article 2 of the 1987 Order), adult training centres, and other premises for the provision of non-resident social services as well as non-residential schools and colleges.

- ### Class D2: *Assembly and Leisure*

83. The D2: *Assembly and Leisure* use class is unchanged. This class includes cinemas, bingo halls, casinos, dance and concert halls, and most indoor and outdoor sports uses except motor sports and those sports involving firearms. Many outdoor sports require the construction of associated buildings, such as clubhouses, changing rooms or viewing

stands, the erection of such facilities would be operational development requiring specific planning permission.

84. Theatres remain excluded from this class. (Note the consequent requirement in article 10, Table, paragraph (v) of the General Development Procedure Order for consultation with the Theatres Trust before granting planning permission on land which includes a theatre).

Nightclubs

85. Finally, the amended Order confirms that nightclubs do not fall specifically into any use class and are *sui generis*. Previously, nightclubs were not referred to within the UCO. Confirming that nightclubs are *sui generis* provides an element of certainty over use as a nightclub and ensures that such premises, which can have significant environmental impacts, are subject to planning considerations before development can take place.

MANPOWER AND FINANCIAL CONSIDERATIONS

86. The changes to the Order are not expected to have significant expenditure or manpower implications for local authorities. Although the increase in the number of classes may result in the need for specific planning permission for a change of use where formerly there was no such requirement, the resulting increased workload for local authorities is offset by the greater precision afforded them in determining applications.

87. Furthermore, confirming nightclubs as *sui generis* is intended to assist local authorities in clarifying a land-use where formerly there was an element of uncertainty. Therefore, the new exclusion should hasten the speed of the planning application process.

88. Overall, it is believed that these changes will help local authorities to pursue their local development framework.

Published by TSO (The Stationery Office) and available from:

Online
www.tso.co.uk/bookshop

Mail, Telephone, Fax & E-mail
TSO
PO Box 29, Norwich, NR3 1GN
Telephone orders/General enquiries: 0870 600 5522
Fax orders: 0870 600 5533
E-mail: book.orders@tso.co.uk
Textphone 0870 240 3701

TSO Shops
123 Kingsway, London, WC2B 6PQ
020 7242 6393 Fax 020 7242 6394
68-69 Bull Street, Birmingham B4 6AD
0121 236 9696 Fax 0121 236 9699
9-21 Princess Street, Manchester M60 8AS
0161 834 7201 Fax 0161 833 0634
16 Arthur Street, Belfast BT1 4GD
028 9023 8451 Fax 028 9023 5401
18-19 High Street, Cardiff CF10 1PT
029 2039 5548 Fax 029 2038 4347
71 Lothian Road, Edinburgh EH3 9AZ
0870 606 5566 Fax 0870 606 5588

TSO Accredited Agents

(see Yellow Pages)

and through good booksellers

ISBN 0 11 753944 9

N177113   C   03/05

£7

www. tso.co.uk

ISBN 0-11-753944-9